DAUNTLESS

Poetry

SHIRLEY SIATON

DAUNTLESS
Poetry

ISBN 978-1-96-105283-3

First Edition, February 2024

Cover design by Artista Grafico
Interior formatting by Mhy San Miguel

Inky Sword Book Publishing
Barangay Quezon, Arevalo, Iloilo City 5000
Republic of the Philippines
inkysword.com

To everyone who believed
It has been a glorious first year
Here's to a hundred more

DAUNTLESS

Poetry

CONTENTS

Part Three: Undeniable

THE JOURNEY

This book was released exactly a year after my debut poetry collection, *Black Cat and other poems*.

The 30 pieces of free-verse poems in *Dauntless* aim to capture my ever-changing world view as a writer and as a woman.

This is a chronicle of my journey as I find my place under the sun and in the shadows. This is where I share the lessons and stories on being unafraid, unapologetic, and, ultimately, undeniable.

UNAFRAID

I hear nothing
Not their taunts
Or wishes for my supposed absolution
I am stone, strong, steadfast
Proud, invincible

DAUNTLESS

I stare into darkness
Wary, watching
Ever so calculating
And cold to the watchful eye

I speak to no one
With nothing to impart
But the blank slate that is my soul
That some say
Isn't there anymore
I hear nothing
Not their taunts
Or wishes for my supposed absolution
I am stone, strong, steadfast
Proud, invincible

I am unmoving
In the rain of time
In the thunder of pain
I am waiting for you
To let me feel again
Breathe again
Live again

DAWN

Eventide slowly falls
Under the stars
That blink and fool
Night becomes my shelter
In this cheerless solitude
Call to me
With your song
Ever promising

Dawn slowly rises
Over my wanting heart
Another waiting chance
For my redemption
Another life
Of nothing and everything
Time flows me by
Ever taunting

Present slowly comes
Enfolding and unfolding
Dawn and dusk
In a circle never-ending
Rising and falling
Eternally, so shall I go
Onwards and seeing

HUNGRY

The sustenance has gone stale,
and I don't want to swallow
perforated hopes that ride
the stillness and the emptiness
as I gaze at you.

Maybe you remind me
that I want to put something
in the void that throbs to be filled
so it can live-
and I think
I no longer want to.

I try so hard
to go down the pipes
like dishwater
when I want to drink you in
as my breath:
I still need to.

REGRESSION

Diverging paths
leading to somewhere
nowhere and everywhere
mud
and quashed
to rain-wet mush.

Singing voice
breaking through
falling and drenching
straggler
and lost
in the vat of destiny.

Striking bolt
tearing apart
into vestiges of what I was
once
and homeward
I plod on.

YELLOW-GREEN

I see the golden rays
glimmer
against my squinting eyes
against the Crocs-clad feet
that wear the pavement thin.

When, walking by,
with olive flesh
and a hundred hopes
and the murmur of second chances—

You look through my
sun-curtained visage
like it isn't there
scribbling dreams away
crookedly
picking the dried grass
to bits.

When you're now
the past
the fallen swipe of life:
you are the veined leaf
fluttering
in the summer wind.

BLUE

Ending in a shattered
pot of clay:
no gold, yet the arch
(seven-tiered)
pours its sorrows
to overflowing.

Pattering on the
stained-glass edifice
of Saints, their halos
threatening to break
from the strain
of false reverence—
the shower
from heaven disbelieved.

Prisms falling
to cut against
cracked skin
with untrue tales
to tell.

When the gray tormented
shall clear away
doubtful Time alone knows;
the blue canvas, white-dotted,
my blinded eyes may
never behold.

FALLEN FRAME

It's time to shut the door
and close it all away.
Since I've lost
what there is
to cry for.

It's time to put the razor blade
back on the shelf
(carefully, as not to nick
 the fingertips with which I write)
and be like a clam:
tightly closed up.

Pry open with the tines,
if you dare,
when no one can.
No one can look
into this little world
and not be blinded.

It's time to pick up
the bits
of the picture frame
that found its way
off the peg.
But the photo's
left unscathed.

SHIRLEY SIATON

It's time to gather
the strewn odes
and flush them down the drain
and shout a slurred
"Nevermore!"
to an unheeding world.

As the fallen frame pieces,
thrown bit by bit
out of the window,
cut into hands
that had brushed away
silent salty rivers.

DELIVERANCE

Away from the entrapment
Of their deceitful shrouds
And prettified lies
It was my time to live
This tribulation is my emergence

Away from being broken
By their enduring falsehoods
And stolen power
It was my time to rise
This tribulation is my odyssey

Away from being destroyed
By the hidden anarchy of old paths
And all-consuming greed
It was my time to strike
This tribulation is my redemption

DISCORD

just like a razor
and its cutting edge
voices and gazes of dissent
slash through my flesh
but never draw blood

the cacophony of lies
from all around
strike greater than a killing blow
I painfully am close by
insurmountable I remain

the festival of unadulterated ugliness
and the breakdown it brings
forces and persists against
my indomitable will
unheeding I remain

DAUNTLESS
POETRY

BLOOD

Thank you.
For the pain
through which I grope my way
in dazed wakefulness.
The void, where
my tongue-tips
catch the essence
of a hungering moon.

Thank you.
For the mead-like meat
of thoughts
long struck by paradox.
Scratching away.
Clawing, until the coagulating life
ensues to stream.
Wanderlust, and more.

Thank you.
For the flesh,
bathed in endless moaning
trembles.
Lined with pain
from endless moaning
trembles.
For the flesh,
seeking the uneven
tease.

Thank you.
For the constancy.
The mundane.
This strange little
taste that leaves
a parched throat half-open.
In expectation.

UNAPOLOGETIC

I will not apologize
For my power
My strength and my drive
For my love
My emotions and my regrets

WON'T

I will not apologize

For my power
My strength and my drive

For my appetite
My ambition and my desires

For my love
My emotions and my regrets

I will not apologize
For all that make me
Me

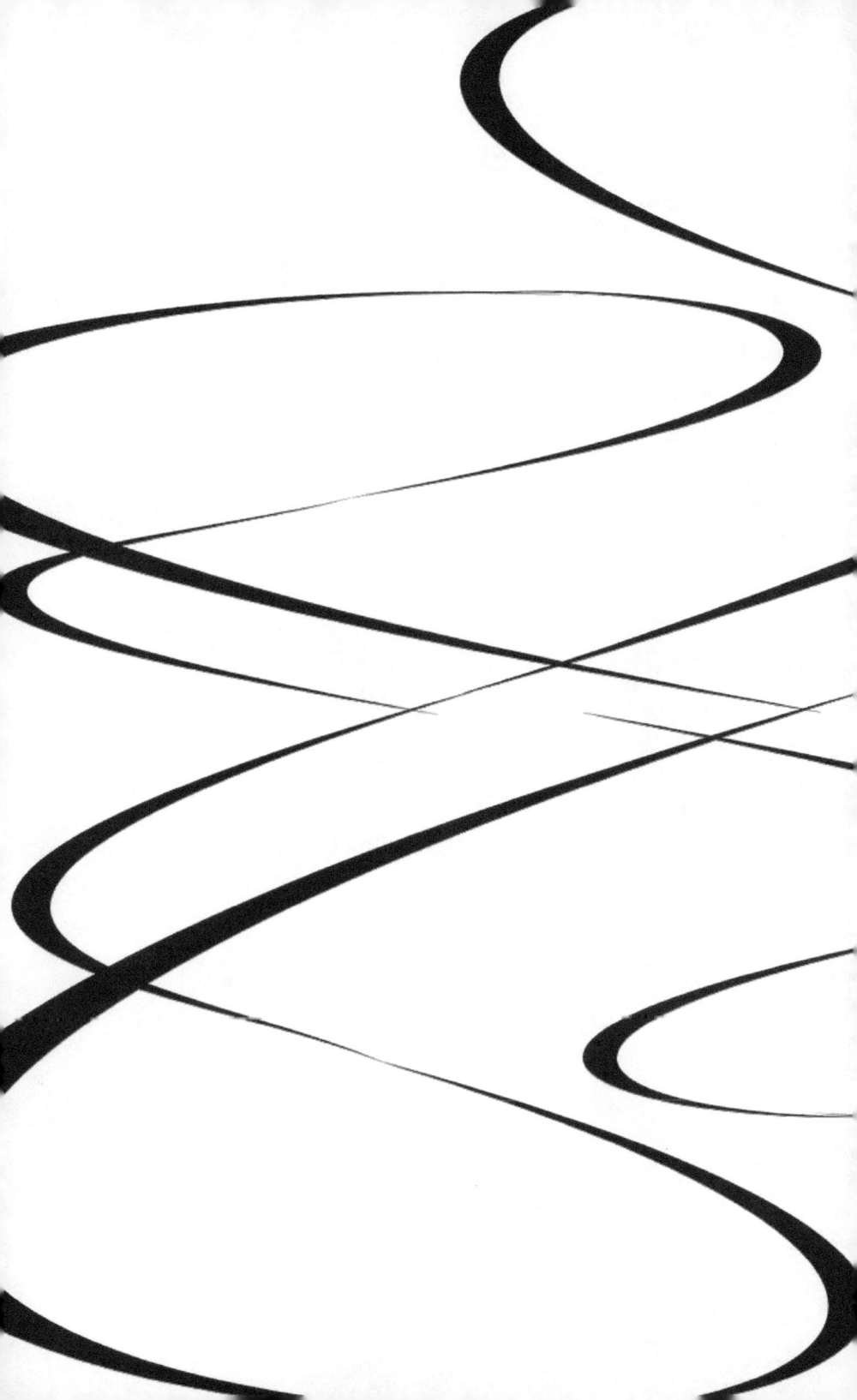

DAMNATION

Every passing second
Is a hateful step closer
To an inescapable fate
Ever reminding
Of Time's irresistible power
Straight on to the very end

Every breath taken
Is made out of desperation
A final, futile bid for freedom
Ever hoping
That the air's purity would cleanse sins
Straight into immortality

Every drop of blood
Is hatefully alive
As it feeds the senses
Ever taunting
With lost chances and hopes
Straight into damnation

DEPRIVATION

There is emptiness
Resting inside my heart
Sitting, waiting, reverberating
With cries

There is emptiness
Thrumming in countless stomachs
Malevolent, ruthless, unrelenting
Eating away

There is emptiness
Shedding darkness on souls innumerable
Plotting, unkind, misdirecting
I yearn to cast aside

DIFFERENCE

As heaven against earth
There are no roads to take
Oceans to sail across,
or rivers to conquer
To bridge the widening gap

As heaven against earth
The land could be so far away
Beyond understanding,
this vicious circle
Of the rise and fall of hopes

As heaven against earth
The golden stairway to the sky
Is but an illusion
a broken promise of salvation
At the end of a rainbow unseen

JUXTAPOSITION

Soar high
in unbounded flight,
tread new-mown blades
with reverence.

'Tis the temple
of olden faith
borne witness
to glory and bloodshed.

With armaments splintered,
was carted away
to watch- and weep-
on the cruel stone stage.

DARK

I hope you will see
Right through the blankness
That is my countenance
It is not emptiness
But a mask of pain

I hope you will hear
Right through the quiet
That is my outward self
It is not silence
But a rage no one will understand
Hence I keep

I hope you will feel
The beating of my heart
That no one knows is still there
I am not stone
Nor darkness, nor torment
I am shadow
Wanting light
I am my unknown self
Needing you

DEFIANCE

 I toil against the sun
As it beats down on me
In an evil haze of drought
Drying the sparse well of hope

I toil against the storm
As it roars all around me
In a vengeful carnage
Bringing death to dreams

I toil against desolation
As its hook cuts into my heart
In irresistible fatality
Denying the bounty of life

DESTINATION

Traverse the ocean
Let my voice swim
Through the rippling waves
Glittering
Beneath the golden sun

Traverse the sky
Let my heart soar
In the sheltering clouds
Embracing
My memories of home

Traverse the miles
That I may be there
Where I am most needed
Choosing
The road of tomorrow

DISRUPTION

i. Lost

Brainfreeze
is all there is to it.
Nothingness
in my line of vision.

ii. Taken

You live in my head
Like cancer
You disrupt my system
As a virus would
A system embracing doom
In unguarded naiveté

You live in my head
Like a dream
You make me waken
In the dead of night
Breathless, empty, wanting
In the unforgiving dark

You live in my head
Like an echo
You speak without yielding
As the unwelcome does
An unwanted temptation
Taking me by storm

iii. Sightings

I am blind
I cannot see behind the mask
I pull over my own eyes
Like a curtain
My mask
My disguise

I am blind
I am bound
By my own darkness
My own unforgiving soul
My own expectations
My pride

I am blind
And I am safe
In this void
Where I remain
Untouched
Untouchable

LONG-LOST TANGO

How Time went past
driving ever southward
like sunbeams
welcoming dusk.

Songs long forgotten
lose what little melody
floating about in dreams—
too worn
from a quest
of finding fragments
once belonging
to you and me.

As the unknown dawns
once more: if we could dance
and know no fear
to the beat
of the long-lost tango.

Even if
scratchy phonographs
play silent music alone.

UNDENIABLE

You matter.

Your art is beautiful.
Your story transcends worlds.
Your voice deserves to be heard.

LIFE

You matter.

Your art is beautiful.
Your story transcends worlds.
Your voice deserves to be heard.

Your hands shape the future.
Your love will make someone believe in themselves—
that includes you.

Your heart beats life.

SOLSTICE

the voice
of a Jack or Jill
echoes
like a song from elementary school
"bah bah black sheep…"
haunting
taunting

"have you any wool?"
none, except what's pulled
over my eyes
with their long standing myopia;
if only the wool
could double as a coat
to ward off
the chill of uncertainty

then again,
the (El Nino) heat
radiates
from my tuffet of safety
where to go
where to go (?)
I no longer know
the spider
I await
to keep me company

"twinkle, twinkle little star…"
things, I no longer wonder
what they are
all are just specks
of dust
in my high-powered vacuum cleaner

a solstice
of worlds that made me
now knitted
like frayed maroon yarn
of a friendship bracelet
I had worn through

a keepsake
enduring
as seasons
come and go

DISTANCE

All alone
In the silence
Of endless thoughts
Poured into an empty page.

The distance: a wall of
Isles, rocks and foam
Travelled on by despair;
Breaking through.

As blood pools
On the scrunched forehead-skin,
The soul had long since
Been lamenting

Chipped away
By time and blindness.
In the other world
It yearned to see.

DIVINATION

See there?

So many visions and dreams
Countless, now formless, pathless
Made and cast out in fearsome ritual
Since time immemorial

See there?

So many souls treading on the roads
Countless, now aimless, hopeless
With minds hungry for enlightenment
Only to be disillusioned

See there?

So much smoke streaming all around
Impenetrable, ever bringing greyness
If only the mist will rise
Give way to light
So we could once more see.

There.

SCARS IN SOLITUDE

Child, let your pain speak
let the scar fade
after the crucible
of silent shackles.

Leaves, aphid-white
drift there- and away;
a hope in balmy
rooms of soot.

Framed lovingly:
twisted images
of lost dreams
grasped in passing.

THE VOYAGE

Cutting through waves,
a swath of foam;
green-gray curdles
trail underfoot.

The raft of makeshift hopes
adrift for days-
and aimless-
steered blindly on.

Beyond the mist,
cobbles and rock-bits
make an inexorable testament
to lands beyond.

A FAT GIRL THING

hanging over
a hunk of ham, of flesh
a slice of the delicatessen
in my fever dreams

slices, and chunks
ripples of sinfully sweet
saccharine and corn
dripping and my senses
peak
(unbearably)

I but pinch my sides
bruised by the too-tight denims
that cut between the cheeks of my
meandering butt

it always hurts like hell
again, and again

as I look at the emaciated
hoochie mamas
with their belly-tanks,
their platform shoes that do not crack
from the burden,
the silver crosses caressing their
firm (upright) bosoms

my hands find the draping tips
hanging over a rolling middle
to squeeze, and squeeze

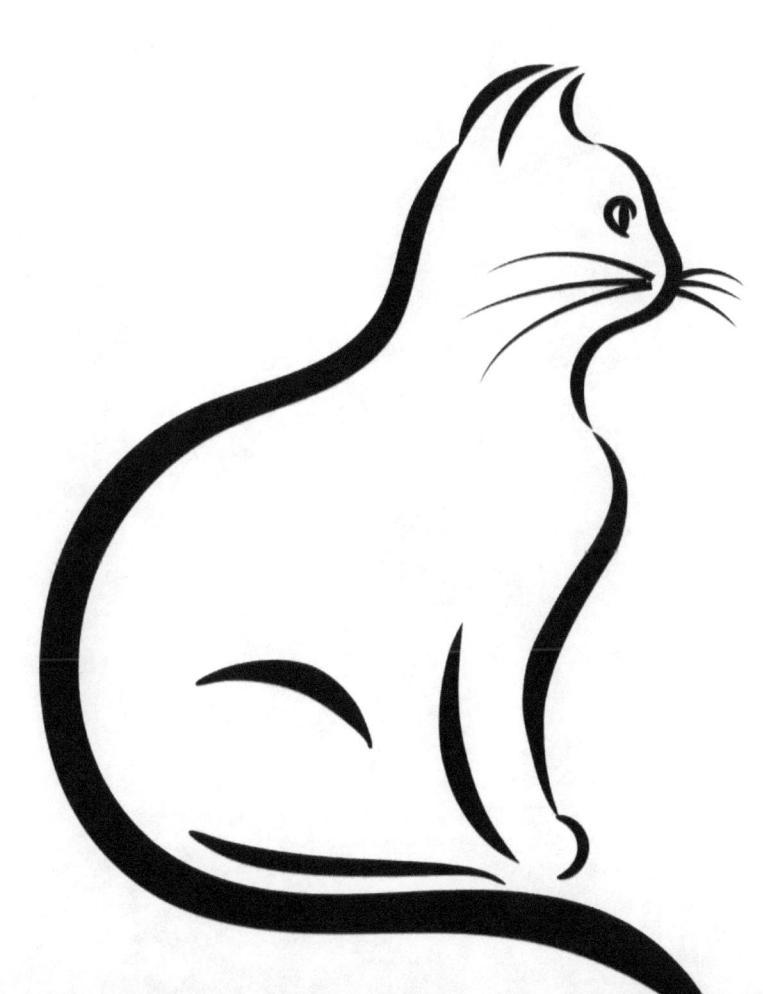

BLACK CAT

Sign of the cross.

It's a phase like everybody else's:
A bit of futile struggles here (I annotate),
sneezy tears there.
Desire is a lollipop I lick at
and spit its taste away.
Only to visit confession
by cutting class.

Don't forget
the dawn rendezvous
of hazy brown-and-white cylindrical pilings
caressing my breath,
of bitter foam kissing
my burning lips,
of heat cascading
down my neck and throat
and chest
and belly.

The water runs over me, to waken.

But then, I always seek
and find
and feel.

DREAMS

It is now time to see
Right through the turmoil
Running its course through our lives
And way beyond

It is now time to break free
Right through the ice
Locking us into a standstill
Forever buried beneath past sins

It is now time to wake up
Bring dreams to life and share a vision
Of our legacy unburdened and unchained
From transgressions past

DIVIDE

I see the world
in a flood of dusty light-bulbs—
A vision pained by Time's merciless inquest
Into a haggard soul;
But I plod onward.

Beneath a skylight
that threatens to cave in,
I bow my head in silent supplication
And my dreams scuttle away
Into the pages of a worn,
forgotten book.

I became a servant:
Hoping, waiting in vain
Until I am but a vegetable
Swimming in a lake of sweat and depravity.

But the dust, too, shall tire and fall
And I will find the light
Streaming—first in puddles,
then in waves—
into my path.

Alone once more, I face
The beginning.
Alone once more, I know
There really is no end.

ABOUT THE AUTHOR

Shirley Siaton writes edgy and evocative poems and stories. Her worlds are in a deliciously dark cross-section of the romance, neo-noir, action, fantasy, new adult, and contemporary genres.

She has several books of poetry and fiction released since February 2023. Her first book is the free verse collection *'Black Cat and other poems.'* She also pens juvenile literature as Shirley Parabia.

She is an award-winning writer, poet, and journalist in English, Filipino, and Hiligaynon, lauded by the Stevan Javellana Foundation, Philippine Information Agency, and West Visayas State University. Her essays, short stories, and poems have been published internationally in print and digital media. Her multi-lingual plays have been staged in the Philippines.

Shirley is a black belt in Shotokan Karate and an international certified fitness coach. Originally from Iloilo City, she is based in the Middle East with her husband and two daughters.

ON THE WEB

Shirley's official website:
shirleysiaton.com

Complete reading guide:
shirley.pub

Subscribe to Shirley's VIP list for free exclusive updates:
newsletter.shirleysiaton.com

www.ingramcontent.com/pod-product-compliance
Lightning Source LLC
Chambersburg PA
CBHW031434120626
46545CB00006B/2405